VISIONS OF THE DROWNING MAN

Other books by Dee Sunshine

The Bad Seed
Dropping Ecstasy With The Angels
Stealing Heaven From The Lips Of God

Dee Sunshine has a website at www.thunderburst.co.uk.

Reproductions of his artwork are available from
www.redbubble.com/people/deesunshine

VISIONS OF THE DROWNING MAN

Dee Sunshine

© Dee Sunshine 2012
Illustrations © Dee Sunshine 2012

First published in Great Britain in 2012 by Skylight Press,
210 Brooklyn Road, Cheltenham, Glos GL51 8EA

All rights reserved. Except for the quotation of short passages for the purposes of criticism and review, no part of this publication may be reproduced, stored in a retrieval system or transmitted, in any form or by any means, electronic, mechanical, photocopying, recording or otherwise, without the prior consent of the copyright holder and publisher.

Dee Sunshine has asserted his right to be identified as the author of this work.

Cover artwork and all illustrations by Dee Sunshine
Designed and typeset by Rebsie Fairholm
Publisher: Daniel Staniforth

www.skylightpress.co.uk

Printed and bound in Great Britain by Lightning Source, Milton Keynes

British Library Cataloguing in Publication Data.
A catalogue record for this book is available from the British Library.

ISBN 978-1-908011-42-8

To my sister **Kaela MacIntosh**

(who once lovingly kicked my arse in the right direction)

The Pavement Artist	11
Autumn In Florence	14
Ecstasies	16
Down To Earth	22
A Burnt Offering	28
Atom Dead Latex	58
The Swimmer ... And She Who Knows	63
Black Night / Pink Gin	69
Bitten Back Words	70
Sledgehammer	73
Rain Of Roses	74
Timeless Moment	75
Holes	77
An Offering Of Flesh	82
In Thrall To Lilith	83
The Blood Of Christ	85
Root Flower Red	87
Days Gone By	94
Slugging For Sweet Jesus	97
Narcissus	98
disOrdered	99
The Pathology Of Love	103
Heavy Weather	111
Vision Of The Drowning Man	120
Afterword	137
Acknowledgements	138
About the author	139

The Pavement Artist

1.

Andiamo! Ho le ali. Andiamo!
Let's go! I have wings. Let's go!

The chalk is ingrained in the grooves of my skin,
a rainbow of pastel dust muddied to iron ore,
the core of me sludge now.

I have drunk drudgery,
through sluggish osmosis become
a cartoon fool in the lap of God, destitute,
a prostitute who sold his soul
for a mess of nickel and gold,
a pimp who put a twinkle in the eye
of too many virgin madonnas.

My knees are calcified, callous
to this pleading pavement,
these pennies not proper payment
for such prostration.

I have lived through
too many winds, too many wars,
my face a battlefield of random colouration –
the pigment, sour and chapped,
my mouth a tight slit
spitting jagged hesitation.

In the beginning I was love,
a conjurer of images which flowed
from passionate heart to jagged hand,
which filled guttering holes
and stilled the wandering mind.

I was in my element,
I was sublime.

But now, it's more than can be endured:
the chalks burn me to cold cinders
and I am no longer inured
to the savaging of time.

Andiamo!

2.

In sleeping, in sinking ever downwards,
in the dull drugged search
for forgotten wings, I am enslaved
to a triple headed hydra
who I can never know:
a bastard hybrid of Leonardo da Vinci,
Botticelli and Michelangelo.

Andiamo!

His clawed fingers
clutched around this brittle body,
my head ground into the pavement,
skull scraped down to a pigment
of polychromatic fury.

      I am the jealous Jehovah
giving birth to a tribe of demons.
      I am the Delphic Sybil
stirring entrails in quicksilver fire.

Per amore, andiamo!

Sketched out on these cold slabs,
I am an icon,
a corpse –
my nakedness an invition
for genuflection
and masturbation.

Here, in my lap, is the Christ child
with lips of lapis lazuli,
a goitred face, sucking all the goodness
from these withering flowers
that once were breasts.

I am a tumbled chalice. I am a kiss.
I am the rust that creeps upon you.
I am cut crystal singing out. I am
rivers running with blood. I am
the apocalpse. I am the flood.

Andiamo!

3.

Such nightmares, such dreams,
to wake from a paralysis
and find you on top of me,
that I am inside you

not being raped by the pope
and a gang of satanic priests —

      I am overwhelmed,
excited, exhausted.

Andiamo!

And yet, nauseated
by the clashing cacophony
of chalk skin against chalk skin,
the smell of copper
ringing from your fingers.

Andiamo!

My head full of sacrilege
as you bring yourself off,
squeezing tight down upon me
like a hot mountain.

Per amore!

And somewhere inside me
an unfelt eruption
as the alarm clock ejaculates
its fascist waking call.

Andiamo!

Our overalls tangled on the floor,
waiting for another day
of uncertain survival.

Andiamo! We must rise up now!
Andiamo! Per amore di amore!

Autumn In Florence

She wears her hair like a halo, a James Joyce madonna,
her Irish eyes spitting fire. Sat opposite is her nemesis,
a perverse shadow-form of the self made manifest,
tempting in her darkness, in her reading of the runes
from chalk scrawls on the wall.

We are sitting in our grape garden:
a walled backyard, a trellis overhead,
heavy with intoxicating, bulbous black fruit;
and I am reminded momentarily of Seamus Heaney,
his fingers dripping with summer's blood,
but more, I think of Hughes,
his Crow mocking us, in our tenuous paradise.

In the bar, wrinkled, walnut-brown men play cards,
the smell of cigars and liqueurs float through
to this backyard, carried on the back
of their sing-song, liquid voices;
a sallow contentment settles, even upon us,
even within our discontented Northern bellies.

In the still, hot air thunderclouds gather. The dark one
is mesmerised: an electrified Durga, she stares into me
with her dark eyes, strokes her fake satin, static skirt;
shimmering with small crimson flowers,
it rides up her legs.
She giggles, as if at a private joke...

And my head dissolves in black, pubic curls of smoke.
I can think of nothing, except of lying expired,
between these too-revealed, summer-browned legs.
The blonde one glares, like she can read my mind...
and she can! She knows me inside out:
I am transparent stuff to her good catholic mind.
I am a nest of vipers, a perfidious prod,
a slack-knickered whore laid out on the altar
of some abominable pagan god.
She stabs her chest four times: north, south, east and west;
she implores the holy virgin to rescue her
from all temptation.

*Meantime, the sun burns mercilessly down,
even through this canopy, and black birds with black beaks
tear viciously at the vine,
raining down upon the three of us,
black grapes from a black heaven.*

In Plaza Santa Spirito I strip off my sweat stained clothes
and dunk myself, half-naked, in the lukewarm water
of the fountain. The sacred spirit doesn't enter me, but nor
do I enter her. I am restrained, if not exactly washed clean
of all my dark desires.

3cstasies

1.

Below the concrete and the flowers,
below the snow and the tubers,
below the moist earth,
below the corpses of broken birds,
below the lava flows and Dante's infernal lament:
the underworld unfolds,
                            eternal and ever-present.

      A different gravity brought us here:
it was not density, but destiny... or so we thought,
sinking down on flustering wings,
alchemical feathers melting in the dark sun.

We were but marionettes, the pair of us,
dancing, hypnotised, on broken glass,
willingly enslaved to Mother Durga
and her Amazing Cascading Circus.
      She taught us tricks, kept us
in her thrall, binding us with incantations
from her big black book.

Here, she said, her voice quivering,
these cards have revealed your tomorrow,
but do not look if you do not want to see
for wisdom brings not just joy,
but bitterness and sorrow.

We were warned;
and yet we begged her to go on...

Then she spilled her box of wonders
on the sawdust circus floor, jewels glinting
in sudden light; and she promised us
gifts that would delight.

These you can have, she said,
these healer's hands, these witch's eyes,
but beware ... for hands cannot heal
if they cannot feel, and eyes that wish to see
must see all, in hideous clarity.

Beware! she warned,
but still we begged her to go on,
laying ourselves naked
across her glittering altar.

She peeled the lids from our eyes,
peeled them off in bloody, ragged strips.

Let there be light! she exclaimed,
and our eyes were aflame.

Then she commanded us to open up our hands
and into each palm with her sacred athame
she stabbed cunt-like stigmata.

Forgive them Lord, she cried,
for they know not what they are doing!

We were undone, awakened to the light
and it was too terrible, too bright;
clutching each other, we wept
like newborns
pushed out of the warm darkness
of the womb, knowing
we could never know
the Tao of absorption.

There, in the acid light,
we could see the door, but could not divine
a way of entering in and being contained...

And how we longed to be contained!

2.

We tasted the light, but tasted it not.
Intangible, it was, around us,
above us, beneath us, beyond us,
but *not* within us.

We should have listened to the weatherman:
he told us dark clouds would roll in –
the forecast was for a fall.

3.

There are simple truths and simpler lies;
and you are anchored by more than you realise
to the treadmill of the familiar.
      Transcendence requires sacrifice:
not just the burning away of dead wood,
but the slaying of all that is known.
      The enlightened acknowledge allegiance
to nothing but nothingness itself.
      They are uncontained.

We were but apprentices
to the burning ladder,
clenching charred rungs,
blowing on scorched hands.
Still, we stretched ever upwards,
nutmeg mystics reaching
for a hallucinated heaven,
clambering up into friendless sky,
high above the safe vaults
of the marshmallow city –
abandoning the shallow geometry
we'd known as home, the safety zone
that lent us definition.

Beyond definition, there is no meaning:
letting go is not letting go,
crashing to Earth is not crashing to Earth
and simple gravity is a simple lie.

Out with the dim-witted banality of here and now,
we are transcendent non-beings:
the perception of our descent...
a mere illusion.

4.

Even within the illusion of darkness,
after the illusion of falling and becoming broken,
we still conspired to breathe together,
to grow together —
our petals glowing with crazy hope,
stamens sending out dizzying opiates
into the putrid air, stems twisting together
in a mocking dance.

*Don't forget, we've seen through
the crack between the worlds,*
we'd say, each to each other.

      But our vanity was in vain
for the few fragments we'd retained
could not be pieced together.
      These bits were just bits,
a scattering of matter,
bereft of meaning;
    they could not be imbued with magic
however manically we waved our wands.

5.

Oh, we clung, like frantic lovers,
each to each other:
desperately trying to blot out
the knowledge of our separation,
each from each other.

In the jigsaw madness of pre-dawn hours
post-coital flowers, heavy and withered,
drift downstream and drift apart:

Slipping into darkness,
        utterly alone,
                I hear your voice,
distantly echoing mine...

A dried out cry
of quiet desperation.

Down To Earth

1.

In the dark aftermath of returning to ground,
our eyes gouged out and our mouths parched,
nothing made sense but blindness and thirst.
Stumbling, raw-tongued, we followed
only the urgent call of need,
the path of simple requisites;
felt out with the roots of our feet,
the seeds of our bellies,
the hunger of our sex.
Smooth and soft to callous fingers,
we were seduced into complacency,
into loving our godless estate.
To be filled, rested, sheltered;
nothing more was required,
nothing more requested.

In the darkness of fucking, we were drawn
to the perilous edge of the sublime.
We loved the danger of sex. The entrapment.
The rent flesh of remembering.
The once upon a time of atonement.
It made our defilement all the more ecstatic.

In the darkness we burrowed down into the ground,
down deep into the moist torpid soil,
through graveyard bones and dense humus,
dead roots and forgotten coins;
through the flaccid vacuous yoni
of the slain hunter goddess.

Here, within the rotted womb,
the corpses of gralloched deer and raped swallows;
a landscape of rusted slippers, creeping ivy,
pools of menses, broken mirrors.

Down, we burrowed; rooting out
worms and small crustaceans, crunching stones
in greedy teeth, feeding coarse bellies,
with no thought of nutrition or digestion:
only of filling holes.

2.

When the canvas of paradise has rotted
and all pigment is bled grey
nothing remains but holes:
      holes that scream to be fed,
      holes that scream to be filled –

filled or defiled

slobbering to polished fantasies
of candyfloss clouds and shredded glass,
distilled toxins and pornographic gloss,
mutilated dreams and Dresden fire...

Love plus fear equals
an impossible equation.

      There are factories spewing out
cleverly packaged indiscrimination
for insatiable consumption.
      In this world of holes, they are the new church:
their mantras mesmerise and stupefy –
a universal barbiturate, casting its grey shadow
in a dazzle of triptane technicolour...
and we are all willingly seduced and deceived.

Holes know only themselves: they cannot conceive
of that which contains them.

Holes know only their pain,
and the constant unfulfilling filling that dulls the pain.
In drugs and sex and television,
in eating and drinking,
in constant consumption, we fill
without filling,
the empty places in our hearts and heads:
obeying the cruel demands
of the fascist in our bellies;
the steel clad Mosley,
the brown-shirted bastard
with the number of the beast
tattooed inside its eyes.

There is no empathy in need:
need will gladly fuck anyone over for a quick fix.

You and I, we learned
the junked out inhumanity of needing:
the chemistry of desperation.
We knew the seed that transformed
      baker into butcher,
      civilian into warlord,
      artist into antichrist:
we knew it in our veins;
we knew it in the choked arteries
of our reason for being.

Having fallen from the impossible dream of flight,
we bought into the supermarket of night.
Cruelty became us, with rarefied ease:
it slipped into our skins,
like a ky jellied cock into a barren cunt.

A Burnt Offering

27th January 1995:
The 50th Anniversary of the Liberation of Auschwitz-Birkenau.

1.

You covered up the mirrors,
not wanting to see the radiance dissipating:
The sexless city sucking you in,
erasing your face.

Without reflection
we clutched at each other:
clinging together like little children.

We clung together
till gravity pulled us apart.

* * *

Junked out on television
we watched the world disintegrating
in raptures of violent dreams:
each dreamer being so much less
than the sum of the parts;
each dream, a fragment
deconstructed from the whole.

* * *

The sirens and screams
that shredded the night's silence
were a forewarning
of the worst that would come.

We could sense the beast's breath
bubbling under the skin of the earth.

* * *

Fucking to the hot dark rhythms of the night
we allowed ourselves the luxury of entropy,
the muted ecstasy of mutual extinction:
it wasn't love, but its fire kept us warm.

    *   *   *

In sleep we would lose ourselves,
let loose shadowy spectres —
abominations that slithered
through the ragged gashes
in the veneer of our sanity;
trailing a terrible afterbirth,
foetid and reeking of fear.

Our dreams gave birth to
       walled in ghettoes,
       bloody towers,
       children without eyes,
       animal corpses,
       beggars, mobs,
       freight trains...
              armies of the dead.

    *   *   *

Waking to the lightless morning:
lost to each other, lost to the detritus
of fear filled dreams,
we would shiver, cling together
and fill each other's ears
with the hot blood
of promised tomorrows.

2.

In holding together and clutching
we imagined ourselves to be whole –
sublimated in a spurious spirituality,
elevated above the chaos of spiky rooftops
and darkly smoking chimneys.

But the sky blew through our every construct,
insinuating a secret hunger, infecting us
with the knowledge of our fragility.

We were held together by mere fragments –
broken pieces that could never be anything more
than broken pieces.

3.

Sometimes, standing skeletal
in the rusted metal wind,
with clouds clearing from frosted skies,
a blur of stars dazzling our eyes,
we would be surprised
by something bigger than love.

Momentarily the futility would fall away
and we'd taste that ineffable no-thing
with an undefined inner sense.

Transcending the linear,
we would cross the border
without passports or maps.

4.

The night before you left
we tore the clothes from each other
and pulled our loins together:
it was a last frantic attempt at connection
before our final separation.

In the deliberate darkness —
      not wanting to see
      what we'd lost in each other —
we thrashed to an angry climax.

You were a Nazi storm trooper
and I, a sub-human Jew.

5.

Last night I sat shivering at my desk
watching the moon track across the sky
listening to screech owls
yammering in the distance,
the wind muttering to the trees,
the silence from my unsleeping bed.

Tonight I cannot pretend I'll sleep.

In the double-glazed safety of suburbia
I cannot excuse this agitation:
these solid buildings nurse the spirit
to slumbering, willing forgetfulness.

But I cannot forget you:
your post-war, housing scheme passions
assail me from across the great divide,
shaking me to my very foundations.

Your ice blue eyes
are watching me as I squirm –
you torturer, you.

I miss you!
I am at a loss out here,
on the periphery of prosperity
with this job, this house,
this security:
I miss our days and nights
of unemployed reckless penury.

I miss the neon emptiness,
the dirty knickers,
the one bar electric fire,
the stinking fridge,
the anonymous screams
in the death still night,
the nightmares
       and our dreams
       of a greener, cleaner place.

6.

My heart is acrid as this ashtray,
hard as blown glass.

There is no poem to our love:
I remember only
the murmuring of your body against mine
in abstract —
        one sideways blow
        and the image is cracked.

I need your hands
to pull me out
from this stagnant murk:

I need your Teutonic no-nonsense
To wipe away this Semitic self-pity.

7.

Tonight I am alone,
with no hand to guide me.

Under my feet
the world is trembling,

mountains are moving
to Mohammed's muezzin call.

Soon the infidel,
will be routed out,

cut down:
devoured in ash and flame.

8.

A postcard from Japan,
a picture of gleaming, erect Osaka —
skyscrapers piercing
a Hiroshima red, sunset sky.

On the back it reads,
*I am alive and well,
if a little shaken.*

My brave, adventuring friend,
but a butterfly's kiss from Kobe:
she says, *don't worry*,
but I do.

Drunk on my father's brew
of cynicism and anxiety,
I watch the storm clouds gathering,
drawing near
and I'm filled full
of wretched fear.

These islands, he once mused,
*are but wretched specks
in a vast wilderness;
and these oceans,
just a dribble of sweat
rolling down the buttock cleft
of an indifferent deity.*

My father knew
the heart of his father God
even before his bar mitzvah day:
he was but ten
when the news filtered through
from Poland and Germany.

9.

The struggle of people against power
Is the struggle of memory against forgetting.
               Milan Kundera

Sleepless,
these flickering images of newsreel
strobe blue in the late night corners
of this hallucinated, tangled room:
random, uncollated images
of collateral damage;
names colliding
in a jangling discordant poetry –

Angola, Sarajevo, Eritrea,
East Timor, Cambodia,
Haiti, Soweto, Kuwait...

an endless litany of forgotten places
like the dispassionate whisper
of a distant, voiceless God.

Here, great Jehovah,
are the bits of a child
who stood on a land mine.

Here is the skull
of a prisoner
who had nothing to confess.

Here are the bodies
of women and children
who were queuing
at the well for water.

Here, there and everywhere
uncountable numbers,
unfathomable numbers:
I would tattoo them
on your loving arms,
dear God.

10.

My great aunt – my grandmother's elder sister –
is over fifty years dead:
no exact record exists,
but somewhere in Hamburg or Hanover
her skin still shades the harsh light of a naked bulb.

Perhaps, that is all that remains of her.

The books that were bound
by the glue made from her pulverised bones
have long since been read and discarded;
and the soap made from her body fat
was used up
scrubbing clean
the blackened faces
of Aryan coal miners.

11.

I learned the necessity of lies early on:
picking up a penny in the playground
there was a momentary flush of joy,
but it was soured by classmates
who gathered round, taunting me,
calling me – *a fucking Jew.*

The half-Jewish blood
in my veins
boiled in shame.

12.

Twenty-five years ago, this very night,
I sat by the muttering gas fire,
in the blue light of the television
and the shadow of my father's chair.

It was then that I hardened my heart,
for I was tormented by his weeping.

13.

Weep not,
for the dead are but dead
and the past is always passing
further and further over
the ever-receding horizon.

14.

Under the eiderdown I twist
like a colony of maggots
eating the last scant remains
of a corpse.

I am cocooned against
the January frost,
waiting for the watery dawn,
wishing this knot of cloth
was a chrysalis —
that I'd burst forth
from these dark dregs
into a wondrous and kindly light.

The clock on the mantle shelf
savages the last vestiges
of the night's silence,
ticking its fascist beat,
dragging me ever onwards.

Malign,
its number fragmented face mocks:
its tick-tock like the rocking of railway carriages
and the tarnished laughter of Polish permafrost;
its hollow echo like the passing of freight wagons
through war torn, crumbling factory towns.

This clock,
with its bland, smug face,
measures the pulse
with the clinical precision of Mengele.

15.

The same sea in us all,
but waves breaking
on different shorelines.

Drunken footfalls
on the stair head
mark the passing
from night to dawn:
the clock laughing,
its hollow pedantry
as celebration reaches
inevitable anti-climax.

I wait for the door to open,
the return of the revellers,
my *sisters* and *brothers*:
one flesh,
but waves breaking
on different shores.

Belatedly, the feast
has been consumed.
Dry mouths have slaked their thirst
with dry waters;

and now the tongues are loose
with burnt offerings
to a dead poet.

16.

Hark, the heroes are returned!
Drunken and clamouring,
their voices raised and roused:
glorious, victorious
and, by the way,
totally fucking stocious.

The Saltire flies high,
blowing in the wind
of nationalist pride.
The Sassenachs
are once again routed:
slain by the true might
of Burns and Bruce.

With haggis and neeps in the belly
and the power of whisky
on their tongues, they ask
wha's like us?
These true blue pure-blooded
xenophobic Scots.

Has the bagpipe's wail
deafened their ears?
For none among them can hear
the same sea
which moves within us all.

17.

It's not as many miles as you imagine
from Nuremberg to Hampden:
the cross is easily crooked.

When the soul is bled dry
there is nothing left
but the braying of empty minds.

18.

Four fifteen, a forest
of broken crucifixes,
flags, effigies,
the reek of stale beer
in half drunk cans:
I fix a coffee
in the crematorial kitchen,
resigning myself
to lack of sleep.

The celebrations are over
and darkened rooms
are littered with snoring:
making my solitude,
my sleeplessness,
all the more poignant.

In the broken wind
I hear black Lilith laughing:
*Schottland Schottland
über alles.
Ich bin unbeweglich.*

Four fifteen and I cannot sleep.
How can I sleep
when you are not asleep beside me?

19.

Back in those halcyon days
when her nest floated upon a calm sea
my mother would lull me to sleep, singing
Silent night, holy night,
All is still, all is quiet.

Back then, I believed
in the perfection of peace.

20.

Finally, I am arisen, like a phoenix
from the ashes of the night:
I wipe the sleeplessness from my eyes
and discard my bleached out, striped pyjamas
in a ragged, loveless heap,
like so much worn out Jew-flesh.

Out the window, the snow has turned to rain
and a thin line of watery daylight
has lain itself across the horizon.

Sat at my desk, I scrape my pen
across the stiff white parchment
of my leather-bound writing book
and cannot suppress the image
of Jewish skin –
        it creeps upon me
with a Semitic tenacity,
sending into the penumbra
any Burnsian sentiments
that might be lurking
in the Scottish parts
of my bastard blood.

21.

Is it my bastard blood
which makes me fear
my country's cry for nationhood?

What is this Scotland?
Is it not just a mass of land,
part of an island,
conquered by robber barons
whose bloodthirsty mouths
declared themselves kings?

Who are these Scots
that claim this nation?
Are they Picts, Celts and Norse?
Britons, Angles and Saxons?
Italians, Irish and Jews?
African, Chinese and Asian?

What line divides
the waves of immigrants
who have settled
on this fragment of island?

Whose hand divines
the right to be?

Who is Scottish, exactly?
Who can call this crag of rock
their homeland…
and for whom will only
arbeit macht frei?

22.

Ich bin, ich bin:
in the loveless dark,
in the icy January rain,
in a silent cold rage;

there is a swastika
where my heart used to be.

My love, my love,
what has become of me?

23.

Weary gunmetal dawn,
a miasma of monochrome:
the wind is stilled
and leaden rain
like dull crystal
softly splinters
on slush stained pavements.

24.

Here I am,
within the soulless framework
of technology,
filled with the rhythm
and hot impulses
of our time.

Herr Goebbels,
your ghost moves
in the salt wind,
whistling through
rusted metal
skeletal cranes,
raw rasping
Teutonic laughter –
Ich höre Sie.

These abandoned docks
bordering the cold wastes
of the northern sea,
my footprints alone
in the grey snow,
but across the waters
and across time,
your voice
following me.

No solace
in the dark sodium light
of this unpeopled hour.

Across the waters,
across time,
your voice is
a thousand broken windows,
a tongue of fire.
smoking chimneys,
a black leather zeitgeist.

From Zyklon B
to bunker suicide –
you see, Herr Goebbels,
tomorrow belongs to no-one.

25.

Among the carnage of yesterday
and the carnage of tomorrow
what hope is there for today?
What hope
for this dismal grey morning?

Without you, my love,
there is no love.

Without you,
there is no God
to oversee this chaos.

26.

These tomorrows, these yesterdays —
if you were here now
they would all be consumed
in the pyre of our passion play.

These flags,
these abstract arbitrary divisions,
would be wiped away.

The slate would be clean:
no scribbled saltire,
no tricolour or union jack
would sully its perfect blackness.

There'd be no star of David
muddying the sky,
no crescent moon.

All would be dissolved
in the fire of our Shiva-Shakti.
All would be undone
in the tender loop of love.

If you were here
I'd be blinded to unbelieving eyes.

No more would I see
this scorched skin,
these skeletons in stained shrouds
of striped cloth.

If you were here
I'd believe in a listening God...

one who heard the trains,
shunting their monstrous cargoes,

one who tasted the sweat,
the sorrow and the bitter ash
of Auschwitz-Birkenau,

one who could conjure up rainbows
and promise a perfect new tomorrow.

Atom Dead Latex

The angels play kettledrums for these dead men:
smiling, sad as colonels handing out medals,
medals for dead men,
medals for warriors who went forth
and multiplied their gift for death,
casting apocalyptic pearls before ungrateful swine,
sowing seeds on infertile ground.
    This is war! All will be destroyed.

There will be no garden of liberation.

A tin machine
        with angry, jubilant, glorious others underneath
        waves in deep trenches of mud:
a second drum-roll of celluloid images
contrived by the avant-garde chosen few,
imagining the burnt out survivors,
their paltry offerings,
their pleading hands wailing.

Now, running away:
not an army, not a parade of green berets,
merely a pawn in the underground,
smelling of piss and fear,
of ammonia and amino acid,
of endings and beginnings.

Soft bellied, raging and ragged,
dragged into the bright
magnesium light,
a death march across the chess-board,
remembering soft, pink milky tits
and being blown to bits –
the wind pushing you ever forward.

Forward by His Light,
this infernal God of Zion,
benignly smiling down
on the broken shell
of this broken town.

Broken and breaking down,
you lie on the roof of the world,
staring down into a white free sun,
high as sky high love light,
white shadows before your body.

You feel nothing
but these pink tit bits,
this blood, this mud:
hear angels singing
alongside the sirens…
   soft and gentle, touching you with their wounds,
drifting like chiffon dressed brides dancing through corn,
drifting like Christ on his cross, illuminating bodies far below
sprayed in meat bits across this charnel ground,
rusted metal dreams unsprung, like tank bits rattling
to the timpani of exploding shell casings,
a crease of cordite
ensnaring your senses.

Such pain in these dreams:
red as aerated blood,
sharp as a cut-throat razor.
   The red leaking out into the soil,
   leaching the body of all vitality,
   leaving it blue as winter's breath.

Hopeless, this dreaming of something white:
hopeless, this dreaming of something soft.
You remember only, how to breathe.

Breathe, nearly naked small boy at her breast,
free like wind, eat up the Earth,
like swimming in warm amniotic fluid.

Sustenance in your belly:
a field-mouse caught unawares,
caught in the snare of your broken hands,
once, so here and now,
now… nothing.
How red meat disgusts!

You remember other times…

Shells exploding all around you,
thick clouds of acrid smoke,

the burning at the back
of your throat.
> You didn't stay
> and die like all the others.
> You didn't talk of home-cooking,
> of cricket matches on village greens.

You said
life is not a piece of cake.

Now you croak, in your blood-gargled throat,
I want out

Sunk down ocean deep
in asphyxiating toxic mud: the corporal cries out
last one into the bunker's a dead man

Bombers pass overhead, grinding the sky
to gunmetal dawn. A second sun
rises in the East. You hear your mouth
leading you down the rutted road
towards death: a red maiden
walking the red squares of the chess board.

You are frightened by these half-starved hallucinations,
command them in a whisper to
Stop

Nothing else: too ragged for flight, too weak to fight.
They strike, like orange-red flowers of death,
like an orgasm of Christ-light,
the swollen blinking of shrapnel,
the thundercrash of the master race.

Death slinks away, leaving moon-craters
in fields of brilliant fertility.
Your legs twitch
with the itch to run away,
but movement doesn't come.

Then a sense of tranquillity descends:
fear backs out the door,
leaving you alone –
a serotonin flood of unexplained joy
lodged in your brain, like a stone.
You sense death approaching

like an aching virgin bride,
her hands outstretched and glowing.
She is Mary, the woman of sorrows,
melting in a river of salt water...
and then she is gone, gone, gone.

Voices, echoing through liquid:
they call you back to the here and now
of corpses and gunshot orchestras,
the serenade of mustard gas
and you replay and replay
the same old worn out can of film –
you are running back
to the small, shelled town
where, only days before,
you were strung out and toxic,
waiting for orders to advance.

You are running back. No fragment of your being
moved to false heroics.
     Absenting yourself without leave
      because you couldn't take leave of your senses.

I am running back

No falling for the stoic myth:
you dream of flying free,
lying in the blood-soaked earth,
under the cover of charred, scorched fronds
that once were crops.

See her coming to you, blonde hair in pleats.
A corn dolly. A hallucination:
the devil dancing on a fiery sea of stones.
Let my hometown fry in a firestorm, you mutter,
grateful for release from this war. Then you see her,
her pink tits milking your thirsty mouth,
an angel emissary of the starving deity:
you hear her bagpipe wail, her disarray,
the mocking cabaret of dead men,
the vile smell of freight trains.

I am nothing, you cry out into the night,
a man-swat fly of fear,
a part of those who would strike out
at a random bunch, a random race...
be they ugly or Christ-like and gentle.

You are running towards faraway hills,
an early small boy naked:
feel nothing now but your lungs...
remembering how to breathe.

Running now, a scream tore her...
to free her breast like the wind,
that you may eat up the Earth.

Her teats like matchwood, leading your mouth to death.
Stones on the red squares of this board.
    Here lies an unknown soldier.
        Too anonymous
           when the orders came in.

Here, there is no garden of England:
no return to the soft rebate of hills,
the rose twines of church gates
and Sunday roast cricket.
        You will never eat from
           these bodies burnt, twisted, torn
                  in soft brown moist gravy,
an idyll of rural angels and chess boards,
red & white gingham of schoolgirl innocence.

This is the wretchedness of all this bloody war:
there can never be a return.

These medals are for killers.

This kingdom, this green and pleasant land,
this happy-ever-after
is a lie, a satin wrapped syphilitic whore.

There is nothing left in this burnt out aftermath:
nothing to breathe;

just this torn pink tit of flesh in your side
(and no pain anymore)

just a choir of vengeful angels
singing you down to dust:
so, you are Christ
and all red meat disgusts.

The Swimmer ... and She Who Knows

Furlong deep in dog mercury cuckoo florid earth,
orange tipped, the swimmer, smeared in dolphin grease,
burrows, scrabbled & scratch-scraped, down
down down
        gulps fairway breaths, rutted,
the imperious, impervious sopping air / downwards,
aching against, seminal gravity of light, dense photons
of ultraviolet infrared x-ray gamma-ed (the stigma skin,
less interesting visually than, say, a Grunewald) / down
against the cuckolded calling of primary, secondary,
tertiary urgency

this not cut, cut up, uppercut,
a stranded dream

breeding false springs, limbs frost riveted to frozen mass /
the swimmer sinking down into darkness /
the man on the radio watching out for swallows,
tit willow, tit willow, the weather diabolical /
thunder, lightning, hail / down into the darkness of dank roots
and wild rubbish / raking among the detritus of forgotten dreams...

and there, he goes relentlessly following her, everywhere she goes;
and I thought we were going to see them mating.

      "Oh, I remember fucking
in the mad midnight winter wheat fields
when I was animal soul, type-writer body,
she was water wheels to my stormy petrol,
and in coitus,
we procreated electric rainbow voodoo children,
cast stratocaster shadows
in the frost of migrant bird workers".

      Down into the stinking earth
where delirious demons mardi-gras parade, fat Tuesday caskets
of pandora miseries / these soul eggs, cracked
in beelzebub's fistular claws /
Eostra promising awakenings
with Christ fasted scientific destructions /
and God is lurking round your bed, like a shadow,
like a thief in the night.

Thrusting through grasping theistic fingers /
sympathy laughing mythological, alcoholic
through mouth-hands, electro-microscopic tentacles
of uncomfortable tradition.

"Is the world a totality of facts?"
Tautologists stare wide through lightless void...
and if God is dead, all sorts of things could be going on.

   Hey, hey, hey, let us look for signs and wonders
in the thunder, miracles in the cracks between the worlds.
Cut up this course now...

miracles are science naturally forgiving,
Will Burroughs and Aldous Huxley in narcotic conflict,
they enable you to heal the nightmare of atonement,
imposing a framework of intelligibility,
a religious impulse in the brain that intrigues
& creation of light is real, unreal, real this world
of information, of growth... and putting our brains
out on the table, you wouldn't be able to tell the difference /
let us blunder through our lives then
with a virtual expression of love / find ourselves
sympathetic to an acceleration
of divine impossibility / the awesome advances
of new technologies / the arch-angel
of silicon based intelligence /
unashamedly millenarian-Aryan /
the drug-taking human mind...
and the unresolved question
of whether everything will shut down
come the tick tock flop into the year two thousand.

I may consider selling my brain /
now that I have been superseded by my computer

And in this crack between the worlds
there are no seamless existentialists /
La Que Sabe leaves a trail of bones /
running with the wolves now / she whispers stories...
and you should listen well, for this crone shadow
is she who knows.

Expressing uncertainty, creeping through the valley,
a possible victim, the wolf –

a common or garden intellectual –
fixes an unreal world in the appropriated arts.
Shamanic & chilled, the quantum multiple-world
anally monopolises imagination.
In and out of belief, the woman constructs
the shiny and bleak details of his world...
black menses of earth / he suffocates /
not waving, the swimmer / computing
the madness of drowning / a fragile thread of hieroglyphs /
perishing in the thin floodlight of moonlight /
he bides down in striations of saturated soil /
La Que Sabe laughing a trail of bones
through bloodless ears.
He corpses on stage / sinks down
into ambiguous nothingness /
a fine spiral of voice, heard only
in the hollows of sleeping hours.

I remember fucking her
in the mad midnight winter of diplomacy:
her foreign office ransacked by floodwaters of union.

He dreams of referenda, drowning in the totalitarian soil
of her wisdom. Her electrical discharges, enlightening
the shadowed cracks between the worlds.
He urges his small fart plebs onto the streets
to raise revolution
and plead for the continuance of darkness,
rallies them with sectarian sentiment.
       La Que Sabe laughs a trail of bones
through the idiocy of their leeched blood /
rapes his bunged ears
with the vaginissimus of her inevitability.
Scalding all tongues
on stolen waters. There can be no sweetness
in the swimming drowning not waving
of initiating patriarch penis wielding God.
       Oh jealous, jealous, jealous,
the infant shielding his scrotum /
brass welded to the cold nothing of control.
The swimmer breathing filaments of earth
into starving lungs.
La Que Sabe waves her breasts in apocalyptic zeal /
the swimmer squeals, clutches the oakwood-iron cross
to his lacerated, sobbing chest.

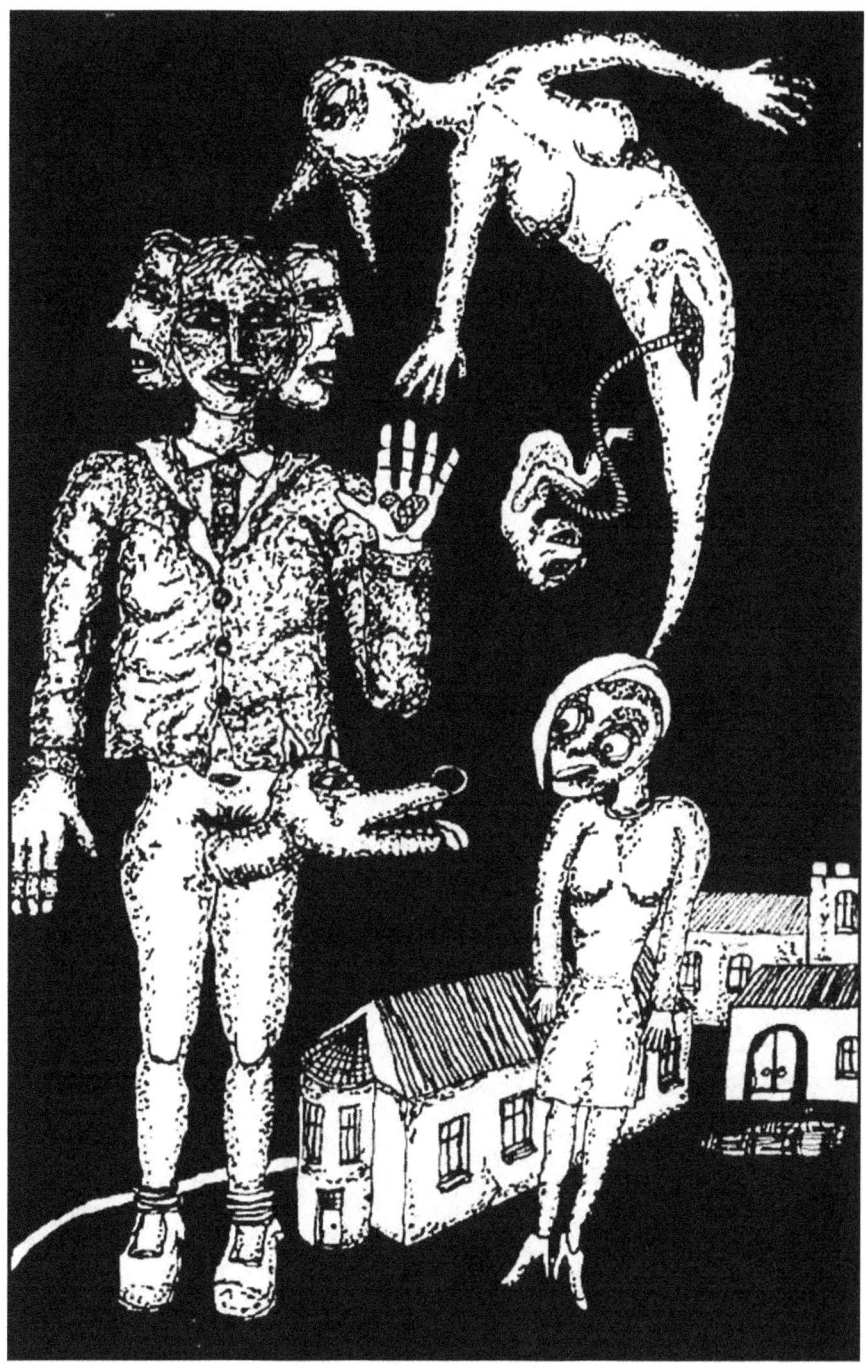

Black Night / Pink Gin

I have lost these bones / scattered them in mad patterns
like a lunatic shaman / out of his mind on iboga,
trying to pull polar-opposite hemispheres
together again.

Saturated in darkness /
I follow the trail as it decays to half-life /
I'm half-dead anyway, grinding my teeth,
listening out for the ghost voice, calling out
to the mother moon.

Mother, mother, the napalm is burning my skin,
burning up within this dead head /
I'm praying to the angels, to take me
to their feather-strewn, unmade beds.

I dream in echoes / treading water
in a quagmire of forgetting /
the mist in wispy strips,
weaving a cloud-shroud round my skull /
I trip through dark tunnels.

Mother is in the garden, yanking up weeds /
pissed on pink gin, screaming sour expletives
at the saviour son / she stares,
dead-eyed at a dead world...

                    ...and she tells him,
it's his fault that she is dead inside / she points
with her dead finger / stares at him, accuses him,
condemns him with her dead dead eyes.

Bitten Back Words

1.

I bite my lips till the blood turns cold,
is blue and bruised, numb with pain.
I bite with all my might,
to prevent the words seeping out:

I know it's time to leave now,
just as the barman calls out
over the foggy river,
drink up please, it's time,
but I prevaricate and circumnavigate
the straightest of obvious lines.

Loneliness is a predatory familiar
who keeps me locked up
in a cupboard full of fear
with whispered threats
of shifting tectonic plates;
and I am hanging on to the edge
of this crumbling comfort zone.

So, I stir chillies into this soup,
to make it taste of something more
than sludge. I wash the dishes.
I take the rubbish down to the bins.
I occupy myself with small tasks,
each step being another step
towards the goal of forgetting.

But still, I remember…

Once I thought you were beautiful,
an angel disgorged from heaven
trailing a comet tail of laughter and fire.

But now you are burned out of all your joy,
as distant and dismal as a fading out ghost.
You no longer smile; and you talk about life
as if it had been foisted upon you.

2.

I'm trying not to remember
this dull parabola, this inevitable trajectory,
trying not to remember
I've been down this road before.

Here, drink this soup, it was made
with something that almost resembles love.
Eat this bird: it never flew!
Sup this pudding, full of artificial sweetness.
Sate yourself with manna from supermarket heaven,
then tell me something spectacular
that will take my eyes away from the door.

But no, I forget, you cannot do that anymore...

Outside, the Autumn wind scours the city,
whipping up the day's detritus in a chaotic vortex:
we pretend we cannot hear it, turn on the television,
turn up the central heating. You crack open
another two beers. "Cheers," I say, my voice shaking
with choked back irony.

3.

In the bathroom, I knock back two blue pills.
They warm the space that lies between us,
the space we used to fill with touching,
the space that was once alive to the cries of coitus.

Softly now, my ship slips into the smooth ocean,
my hand forgetfully brushing
the soft cleft between your pyjama legs.
You jerk in your sleep, turn over, turn away,
leaving me alone and frightened
until the darkness eventually envelopes me.

Sleagehammer

I wet my finger,
trace a line through plaster dust:
expose the raw, rust-encrusted metal.

Metal and plaster taste in my mouth.
Yin to yang —
plaster submits to metal,
implodes to its shiny touch.

Where once there was sculpture,
now there are only lumps and dust.

Metal and plaster —
the taste is tart, wry and sexual,
filling me with its corroded essence.

Tonight I want her very much.

A Rain Of Roses

I fell from the sky,
blazing a trail
of violent flowers:
orange as caesarean sex,
red as shiva-shakti,
crimson as you,

my petals torn away
in the scorched wind,

mad mistral mistress,
you plucked at me
with triggered fingers,
till I was
but dry stems
and withered seeds.

You plucked
and I was undone:

I fell to the ground,
a dust of forgetting,
smothering crops
and blanking out the sun.

A Timeless Moment

Your surrender to me
is the ultimate sacrifice:
you are the O of every orgasm
and the M of every mantra
that has issued out
of these scowling lips.

I love you
for letting me enter your past,
for letting me slither
through the O of your beginning,
for absolving me
in the dark pinkness of your womb.

You are
the ultimate manifestation –
you lover, you mother,
you murderer!

I lay myself supine at your altar,
worship the glittering menorah,
incandescent in your eyes.

Your face
is a thunderburst of falling stars.

You are the universe, this moment,
and this moment is all there is.

We are timeless
in this placeless place,
I drown
in the salt sweetness of you;
you witch, you nurse,
you goddess!

I am rapt:
a ship drawn to the siren rock;
a fool, one step too far
over the edge of the cliff.

Your arms are every place I am,
your road is the only one I know;
you Sheila Na Gig,
you golden thread,
you weeping Ariadne.

We are one,
Hermes and Aphrodite
suiciding our selves
in the name of each other;

widow and widower,
apostles of the moment,
ragged to the rapture,
caught in a loop of ecstasy.

I cry out and you cry out –
your terror, your elation,
your despair…
          like we're fucking
on the edge of an abyss.

Holes

Cigarette smoke hunkers round the angle-poise,
a vile yellow fog thickening the air, congealing
your thoughts: you want / you do not want,
the words slowed to meaninglessness
the sluggish sound of them sucked in
with each tight nicotine tainted breath.
   Wanting... like the empty ache
after masturbation,
the hole that will never be filled.
   Wanting... you feel
the wantonness of it in the pit of your belly:
a hunger that drives snakes to eat their tails.
   Wanting... you know it in the darkness
of the dark hole below:
fucking and being fucked,
men, women, images, demons;
you've had them all...
you have filled and been filled,
but never have you been fulfilled.
Never, until now, you think, maybe.
Maybe, shaman raking your way
through a fragmenting underworld:
crawling over sharp, broken things;
china doll parts, razorblades, watch springs.
   And for a moment there,
   you realise
   you are truly revolting to yourself.

What is this love you think you feel?

You love her / you love her not.
The questions plucked like petals from hemlock,
you nibble them with the puckered lips of the connoisseur,
the gourmet who has had too many holes,
the salt-earth aroma of them conjured up
like so many words –
   small, tight holes,
   hot wet holes,
   holes of every taste and texture...
   like wines, you can describe
   every nuance of their flavour.

But what is this love you think you feel?
Something beyond the boredom of fucking:
the endless, but compulsive dinner of nothing?
The realisation that you are revolting to yourself?
The desire to transcend the banality of simply being?

You love her / you love her not.
The image of her with briars of blue cornflowers
woven through the sunlight gold of her hair.
You ache to touch, to stroke the downy cheek,
the crook of arm, the blush of freckles:
to sink into the dark, endless blue of her eyes.
Longing, wanting, needing.
You love her / you love her not.
The water of her
turning your headstrong planets top-heavy,
spinning orbits of chaos. You have never felt
as deliriously delicious as this,
not even at fourteen,
with unrequited lust painting pastel fantasies of love.

You love her / you love her not.
How many times have you had your hole and felt nothing?
How many times have you clung to the shores
as the rip-tide dragged you under?
All that flesh, all these holes...
All those dangerous nights turned to nothing.

She has destroyed everything:
this Kali Ma dressed in blonde softness,
with her breasts of sweetened, poisoned milk.

*　*　*　*

Midnight.
The hours spiral away in narcotic confusion,
the clarity you sought to possess eludes you still.

Another pill?

As if you could tear salvation from God's winking eye:
the God who comes only in moments of despair,
the God who couldn't care,
the God who was never there...
       except in a stranger's embrace.

The telephone is hot vulva pink.

You *could* call.
But not before you know
whether you love her or you love her not.
        She's ruined everything:
        turned flesh into mere flesh,
        holes into mere holes.

Black midnight, the city pulses with sex:
Saturday night prowlers and ghosts
seeking their own extinction
but tonight, you are separate: outside,
watching dispassionately,
as the strangle tango begins the process
of its own completion.

Another pill? You think you will:
something to see you into the sober light
of Sunday morning,
something to lead you to comprehension.

Meanwhile the ghost of you haunts the pick up joints:
tequila rapido, absinthe, after shock, cocaine,
leading you on to the inevitable expiation of flesh.
Is it too late to get your coat?

Ghosts.

But you cannot leave.
The telephone is hot vulva pink
and *you love her / you love her not.*

The moon tracks a slow arc across the sky,
bodies briefly couple,
orgasms ring out into a void of impermanence,
atoms disperse and reform
and then, all are sullenly alone.

Your cock presses hard
against the dark cotton of your trousers:
all that fucking,
all that knotted, sweating flesh...

And yet, so desperately sad.
Your fingers cradle your balls,
comforting your world weary soul.

You slow-dance solo through the schizophrenic night:
the half-eaten moon calls, cold and white.
The telephone is hot vulva pink, tempting your fingers:
Across the city,
seven digits away,
she is naked, warm, willing,
waiting for your loving.
She loves you / she loves you not.

When you think of her, it is more than tits and holes.
She's the home you've been seeking all these years.
She is the moon, she is Venus, she is Mars.
She is a countless number of distant stars:
a scattering of light that turns the sky away from night.

And now everything else is corruption and rotten flesh.
You love her / you love her not…
remembering the taste of her, the touch of her:
angelic, golden and clear,
as if she were made from finer dust.

      *   *   *   *

You imagine her petrol blue eyes,
the clouds passing away,
a clear and calm day,
the fruit of the forbidden tree,
a forgiving God,
a pink telephone,
a harbour of still waters,
the touch of her fingers on your chest,
the crinkle of her cheek as she smiles,
the smell of summer,
dandelion fairies blown in the wind.
She loves you / she loves you not.
She loves you / she loves you not.

Her petrol blue eyes:
you drown and you burn,
the spectre of flesh.

How can you love her and love her not?

    *   *   *   *

Hours into the morning, nothing is resolved.
You love her / you love her not.
A sleeping pill for each which way:
you slide under the duvet, alone and lonely,
your fingers cupped round your balls; chaste, safe –
the marshmallow wonders of chemistry
dragging you out into the warm dark seas.
You love her / you love her not.
Sinking into dreamless sleep,
tomorrow is a hundred million light years away.

An Offering Of Flesh

She was hands and claws groping, harsh
in the neon back room, her flesh
sweating sugared wine and cheap perfume.

Tell me what you want, she said,
tell me what you want, but I was too drunk
to articulate the raging of all my dreams.

The sourness of age trembled
in the tracery of lines on her face.

I listened hard to her breathing,
I listened hard to the movement of her tongue,
but still I couldn't hear her story.

We coupled:
lost ourselves in folds of caustic flesh;
strained violently towards unthinking oblivion,
the blankness of orgasm,
the wet mess of biochemistry.

She came to me like a sacrificial lamb:
her powdered scented flesh, an offering.
She steered me through blurred corridors
and took my fingers in her mouth,
promising sweetness I had never understood,
her eyes full of all the sorrows of the world.

I wanted to give her a fix of joy, to bathe her
in the cold sharp exhilaration of life, to fill her
with more than just moist emptiness.

I wanted to untangle the barbs,
to loose the briars, to heal her wounds.

She was a Christ, a Madonna, a Magdalene:
the blood of saints stirring inside her skin.
She was a sacrament,
a Goddess who extinguished herself for love
and she was sorely mocked for all her giving.

In Thrall To Lilith

She parades into my dreams: her impudent pudenda,
an open, intricately carved flower.
Bees and stinging things live within,
waiting for the soft whisper of invitation. She is…
vinegar and vanilla, vaseline and vagina.

She is a cascade of vocabulary: vibrant and vivid:
the supreme vivisector of vacuous idolatry.

Her dictionary is a thrashing of ten-fold limbs;
and all meaning is encoded
in the fluttering of her labial wings.
I am a prisoner to her intelligence,
her volition, her erudition.

There are pale blue men
working her Siberian pits,
freezing;
and all for the want of a kiss.

Lying out on her gypsy brass bed, she smokes a cheroot:
staining the walls with disdainful agitation – her cheeks,
red as those of Modigliani's whores.

The blasphemies of pigment beguile:
viscous rivers drain the soul
of every homely warmth.
Her likeness cannot be caught:
it eludes with simplistic ease.
Teasing, she baffles me
with the pink virtuosity of her tongue.

In vain, I reach out to grasp her grassy banks:
yearning for the safety of a foreign shore;
the heat of inevitability,
the dark depths of her cavities.

It was she who devoured my strong ancestors:
she who left Christ crying and gasping for breath.
What hope then for me,
with only my clotted paintbrushes
and second hand adjectives
to protect me?

The future, I see, is a glassy cold pit:
yielding nothing more
than small handfuls of flawed diamonds.

The Blood Of Christ

I am drunk on the blood of Christ and the rain
is playing a Mississippi swamp trashcan beat
on this caravan roof.

You would not know me now.
I am vacant:
a vagrant drifting through fifteen fictions,
fifteen different versions of myself.
Today, I am a desolate Kerouac,
mouldering away in these northern wastes
after avoiding a romantic death.

> I am:
> my typewriter rusting
> grey clouds of paraffin vapour
> cigarette smoke
> the cloud soaked sky
> a blackbird singing in the sodden pine
> the smell of her on my fingers.

The smell of her on my fingers, unwashed
in the wake of a week of sex:
> my senses have been re-awoken
> and I haven't got enough fingers
> to plug up all the holes.

Her absence was not felt before.

I was inured / insured against all emotional intrusion:
grey as paraffin vapour, grey as cigarette ash,
grey as incense smoke...
free of confusion,
here, in the ribbon glens that snake through
these god-the-father, great-spirit mountains.

I finger my holes:
there is a rawness verging on pain.

If I poke some more
maybe something red, soft & vulnerable will issue out:
something sweet and intoxicating
like the blood of Christ.

Her presence was not felt before.

In the prowling of our sex
we explored underworlds:
the drumbeats of some dark unspoken.
She was a she-wolf shaman,
a hybrid of every mythological woman –
she undid me.

I bathe my fingers in the blood of too many saviours:
damned by the opening of too many eyes, too many holes.

The smell of her:
it lingers on the tips of each of my fingers.
Mississippi mudflats under each of my nails.
I was Huckleberry Finn to her Uncle Tom,
Mister God to her Anna.

She undid me
and left me pondering over all the broken pieces.

And then there was the war on my radio.
She said:
*here comes the apocalypse,
and so I kiss you on the lips.*

When she came,
a sky of missiles scudded the oil black soil of Iraq.
When she came,
Jehovah and a nest of snakes exploded in my head.

And when she went, I realised
I had been one of the quietly anxious,
      semi-animated, living dead.

Now, the war is almost over:
the conclusion, an inevitable anti-climax.
The world continues sleepwalking and stumbling on,
drunk on the blood of too many Christs.

I have no more alibis. I am undone:
as empty as a caravan shell on the edge of a bloated loch.
I wish the rain would wash me away.

These holes are too tender:
the grape of this wine, too bitter;
and the days too long, too wearying without her.

Root Flower Red

1.

This flower is fire red,
a core of vermilion,
petals petulantly open.

Within the folds of stamens,
filaments and fuzz
is a centre of cunt;
a descent into primal void,
into primitive violent being.

The taste of it
in the mouth
is sour, musty, intoxicating:
the taste of blood
pulsating to the ululating tide
of the moon.

2.

What I mean to say though,
writing in the dust with bones, is...
my dreams are peopled with holes:
tunnels, entrances, openings;
a crazy paving of windows and doors.

I am constantly a victim of movement,
squeezing through constrictions,
falling or flying through dead, silent air;
and in my dreams, always
I awake to the ubiquitous wan, grey light
of sleepless morning

yawning

scratching armpits, face, thighs,
rubbing never-quite-awake eyes:
the petals of yesterday like dust
to the rusted clock's restless ride

And what *is* on that other side?
An unattainable, unimaginable light!

3.

Through this blood flower,
through the angry vibrant red of it,
the root of our collective being,
the root of our animal soul,
we struggle towards the light.

It is no accident
that this spectrum starts in red.

We are all blood:
cunt, cock,
meat, flesh;
intestine,
artery,
vein.

4.

To dive into red
is to be swallowed by cunt

to relive
the clamped agonies of our birth

in anticipation of death
and the ultimate constriction
from which there is no release...

death is the place
we have truly learned to fear

suspecting there is
no hallucinated rainbow,
no fantastic flight...

only unspeakable blackness:
a void,

the ultimate negation of light.

Days Gone By

Androgynous, ambivalent:
this perpetual twist-shifting, down the chapel
on a polluted October blustering impossible morning...

She condenses all thought, all feeling, into similes
like butterflies caught in a web of clichés –
it's easier that way.

       Albert walks meandering thru' W12, proud as
cactus hairs, a twine of Verlaine in his cock pocket:
prole voice pole-vaulted thru' distant clouds
but he has never seen one up close –
airplanes, cocktails and dark sentiments don't mix:

Albert is a man
with his feet on the ground.

       Anodyne & alert
       she sucks his dull prick

The penis, a hairless cactus plant
in the desert of her lonesome old soul.

But the poetry of penetration is a complex issue
and the rubbing of dry tissue,
a mere catharsis
and Albert,
a man with his feet on the ground.

    *   *   *   *

in algeria, on a clapped out remington rand,
with syphilitic ten year old boys
lounging about in his back yard,
he explored a netherworld
his beatnik friends only dreamed of...

but that was way back when
before the shepherd's bush
of altered realities
shrunk into flatline banality

    *   *   *   *

In the cloisters of 49 Adelaide Grove,
after the short dark walk from White City,
he enters her: a stranger, an envoy,
a messenger; he reads aloud
passages from People's Friend,
rocks her to sleep with his laughter.

Drifting off,
on the magic carpet of her laptop,
he calculates
the days gone by.

There
in the clock gland,
in the clenched fingers of his right hand.

Sometimes he imagines
the spectre of Edvard Munch
painting a giant vampiric cunt:
the image makes him smile,
even though

he is dried out, desiccated –
a misanthrope
hung by his own rope.

    She smiles into her knitting
    and he is compliant,
    silent tap tapping
    on her laptop,
        a spew of words,
        a senescent recalling
        of these days gone by.

    *   *   *   *

algeria is a dream of dark red blood:
mirrors speak of
    vulvas and vestibules,
    labyrinths and monsters.

she winds the clock, but not back.
peeling away labial lips
she smiles,
like a score of young sun browned boys.

   * * * *

And then they are a fusion of cock and cunt,
an extinguishing of all distinction.
Into nothingness they fall,
clutching
each to each other.

And then there is that insistent voice,
throwing questions at your feet:

What flowers express
     days gone by?

And you know the answer:
it's as clear as a Fassbinder film —

Lilies,
white lilies.

   * * * *

Hands soft as bread,
Albert walks thru' a monochrome forest.
He arrives at a clearing
and e-mailed to him
in crystal clear chromatic colour
is a jpeg file of a florist shop
spilling over with white lilies

and attached to them:
the love note he never wrote,
which he had hoped would express...
days gone by.

Slugging For Sweet Jesus

Slugging for sweet Jesus,
the benign smile melting us to stupefaction –
a crucifix draped round your neck,
diabolically pressing its lascivious fingers
into my needy flesh.
          This thirsty skin, crying
for the rough thrust of sublimation.
I want, I need... transubstantiation,
justification, a fix of revelation,
the smell of your male flesh enveloping me.

You can play Rimbaud to my degenerating Verlaine:
pierce me with your vision, fill me
with your terrible work.

A shrug of ether, a pinch of sulphate –
my love, it is late! Let our raiment fall from heaven,
let the clouds in my head enfold us.
We can fly to the hot South and share our wings.

Trousers round my ankles –
the metal of you inside me, churning my viscera
till I am so soft I fall.

And in my sleep, away from the sugared hell
of this anonymous Chelsea Hotel,
I dream of Armageddon and the Cabaret Voltaire –
the seven angels of the apocalypse
concocting a cacophony on harps and horns,
the devil on the slide trombone,
a toothless old voodoo man on the drums,
dancers moving like grease through a sewer,
smiling insanely, with petro-chemical rainbows
on their faces, Dali, dressed as a magician,
ejaculating faeces from a top hat
and throwing melting clocks into the numberless void,
Marcel Duchamp walking forever naked,
up a stairway backwards...
and even in my drugged out dreams,
there is the rhythm and the heat, the constant beat
of your never satisfied meat
inside me.

Narcissus

Tense as fisherman's reel, irrigating dry furrows deep
into gnarled roots, scratched and acid etched /
anxieties and misconceptions disconnecting spirit
in tarnished dull silver spirals, silted canals, cracked
craniums, depleted uranium, a half-life half lived /
rigoured bodies ossifying in isolated vile madness /
pulping your liver in masticating teeth / emasculating
yourself without the usual misogynistic assistance /
you crawl through an oedipal underworld, an Orpheus
spell bound by flickering television light / a web of
black Lilith's spells woven round your panicked head,

    fragmenting
        fracturing
            splintering...

You are a dichotomy, an anomaly: an idiot
on a ship of fools; you levitate and fall; crashing
through the cotton candy fog of mindless mind.
       Soft as pus, you sag, ragged and sunken:
a doll-form with big doll eyes.
       Love me, love me, love me, you cry, semen
arcing in parabolic, diabolic flight; and you implode
in the ashes of night – a quantum step away
from the epicentre of your being.

Dissolving in the boiling cauldron of the crone moon,
all sense of self: you erase all memories,
like so many bar room brawls and midnight fucks;
slamming tequila in the lowest circle of hell, with
Dante by your elbow whispering red flashbulb light
into your retina...

A soft vulva hotly enfolds you.

disOrdered

dAdA scrambled: too late this night.
No *you* to superglue the bits together
so, destined to drift aimless,
frameless,
thru' the remaining years
contemplating
razorblades and pills

but
undecided & too scared.

An emotionless voice in my head
plays in an endless loop:

Why kill time when you can kill yourself?

Wondering
who you are fucking tonight,
this night,
as the bed beckons:
empty and unforgiving…

If there was someone, *anyone:*
doesn't matter who…

Just someone to hold my hand,
stroke my fingers till I fall asleep
till the blankness swoops down
and devours me / till I am deVOID
of all these X-S emotions.

Meantime,
Kurt Schwitters is building
a random construct
in my small intestine:

not that I am exactly hurting,
not that I am missing *you*…
not even the bitter musk scent
from the crook of yr neck…
or the soft contours of yr belly…
or the wry twist of yr smile…

or the ink stains on yr fingers...
or the wistful look in yr left eye
when you waxed euphorically,
full of bitter-sweet *one-days*.

No, I never loved yr idiosyncrasies,
I never swooned with lust
to the lyre-song
of yr own peculiar idiolect.

This is false memory:
out to destroy the delicate balance
of my being-here-now-ness.

Some nights
the loneliness bites
chunks out of my brain.

Here & now,
I have not sunk *that* low.
I am mindful of my breath,
if bereft
of *metta*.

I breathe into my hara
and the illusion of tranquillity
is made manifest:
black and dense as syrup.

The emergency exit sign glows,
liquid crystal green
and so seductive.

Remember,
even the Buddha
tried to waste himself once.

He said:
paradise is for humming birds and fools.

Counting the breaths,
the minutes, the hours, the days:
I perceive myself to be
beyond redemption.

No insipid Christ could carry me.

I am a slut to my expectations:
will spread my legs
for any worn out old promise.

One, two, three, four, five:
once you caught a fish alive.
Six, seven, eight, nine, ten:
then you let it go again.

Not waving, but drowning:
a fish-hook thru' my cheek,
just under my right eye

Counting the hours till daylight
the samhain moon
burning thru' the windows
into the dull kernel of *me*.

La bella luna
pregnant and laughing:

she who oversaw
our first velvet velcro fuck –
galaxies bursting
out of your eyes,
filling my dull room
with wondrous incandescence.

Where are you this night?

Are you extinguished
like some overburnt candle?
Does yr beautiful head nestle
into yr lover's soft belly?
Do the pair of you smile in your sleep,
like cats that have had too much cream?

There are three nightlights
guttering in my window
to keep the witches at bay.

I stand in tadasana,
trying to find my balance:

I'm a tree
blown in random winds.

I breathe slow and deep into my hara:

still counting,
but the moon hardly moves

stirring a longing
in my belly.

The Pathology Of Love

1.

He is psychopath.

He wants her love *truly madly deeply*
delights in strata of pain she inflicts...
her brown eyes, twinkling cesspools,
her orgasms quickly bought,
a supermarket of vengeful menstruation.

She is angel to his masochism.
Shit on me he begs,
but she will not stoop to his pleading,
making his humiliation
so much more poignant.

2.

4am
she speaks into his answer-machine,
leaves cryptic messages, suggestions of *love*

hints that she might give over a small slice of herself
for his safe-keeping.

Her voice burrows, like a parasite,
into his slow panicked waking.

She rings off with psychic alacrity
and will not respond
to his constant ring-back requests.

Oh the sweet agonies of too much love!
He is besotted with the idea
that he might never sleep again.

Love is an angel, bottled in frosted glass.

He heaps presents upon her,
suffused with television tenderness.

She bins everything he brings,
laughing (with lilting, intoxicating voice)
she informs him... bringing him
to a violent climax of delicious agony:
he could not be more humiliated
were he to walk down Sauchiehall Street
saturated in stale semen.

3.

She is sociopath.

She perverts his dreams with 4am panicked calls,
feeling the insecure threads of her treading water-ness.

Her other lover has cut away, revved up outboard escape and she is overboard and panicking,
needing to be reassured...
but the fucking phone is not not not doing her command,
so she throws it out the amphetamine tripwired window
into the Camberwell neon darkness
to cacophonic chords
of trip hop jungle ragga.

Water will not balm her,
nor the arms of an adoring-someone calm her.

She cannot sleep for the chemical shite
in the sewage pipes of her veins.

She contemplates razorblades and all sorts,
while listening to Björk,
the CD on a constant loop of repeat
until dawn swallows
the last of the night.

4.

He is idiolect.

The semantics of masturbation
lulling him to sleep.

Little fucking scrubber he thinks,
exhilarated by the illusion
of pornographic mastery:
he is an idiot slave.

He slathers like a lobotomised hound,
into the grey underworld of nothing.

Love hath his hands fetter bound.

5.

Light is not enlightenment.

Richard & Judy cunt-manipulate her into placidity:
life becomes... just so...
a Coronation Street corona of smiling complaisance;
all problems reduced to a lack,
filled by product
and prozac.

And then she is crashed out
on the aquamarine velour-covered settee;
dreaming of wedding cakes, blushing boys,
a universe collapsing in simplicity.

Then she comes upon
the well at the end of the world
where the sweetest, most palliative waters are drawn,
but if stolen
shall surely put out
the fires of heaven.

Heavy Weather

1.

Into the darkness,
into an envelope of lacquer black cloud,
this ship slips, spinning starboard arcs
of star-sparking, primeval chaos:
a distempered soup sludge
of unresolved, unfettered emotional detritus.
Here, this here, in the belly of Saint Paul,
the dust of the Damascus road
under these chewed fingernails.
      Too long, I've been waiting
for the blind sunburst of Christ light…
it no longer matters
that a few of these followers
may yet get put to death.

Meanwhile, in the boardroom,
there is talk of sailing bravely on…

The bilge is clogged, bulging pregnant
with the eternal sweetness of stolen waters,
a catacomb of rust flakes
and rainbows of hydrocarbon.
Slowly, slowly, I am digested
in the ulcerous belly of Saint Paul…
bailing out with pierced bucket
& flailing windmill limbs.
      Here, a rage of impotence in this coffin.
Here, in this underworld, where choleric fevers
bring on intemperate hallucination,
I am sinking down, as I must,
into the black waters of Dubh Uisge.

We are led bravely on,
the sails billowing in a Capricorn wind.
We savour the faint scent of cinnamon,
of cumin, of lemon grass
& give praise to the myriad gods
who live under the ocean's skin…

Soaked in acid spindrift, I lie out flat on the deck,
dreaming of brave new worlds.
I have seen gleaming white towers
and soft blue rivers carrying cargo boats
of smiling, sun-tamed tourists.
I have seen a sky that would pierce your eye
with its ineffable beauty.
I have seen a cascading kaleidoscopic circus
of tempestuous yearning.

Saint Paul is in my belly, waiting for God:
spiking these stolen waters
so that they are not so sweet.

I remember what she said
about waiting for storms to pass.
I remember the cold balm of her lips,
the shaky brush-strokes of her hand,
the sweet and sour acrobatic contortions
of her mind, the pink sweat of her sex.
I remember her.
Oh sweet Jesus,
I remember her too much!

The Captain says: here comes the big one.
The Captain says: we're all going down.
The Captain says: you'd better pray
 your kingdom will come.

Tidal waves can wash away the bravest of cities,
can make a mockery of the most earnest intent.

The river's tent is broken.
Once again
our faces split open:
our dreams
scattered to places
we cannot map.

So that's it, we're all going down:
down into the foul, rotten ocean –
this ship of fools
in the belly of Saint Paul.

Oh Jesus, Oh Mary, Oh Mother of God:
forgive me for pissing on the angels' wings;
forgive me for burning out
in a spiral of falling stardust flame;
forgive me for wishing up the amber ocean deep –
these waters which reduce
even the strongest of edifices to sand.

Once I was colossal:
proud, erect, perfect.
I adorned myself
with gems and precious metals
that shone like the voice of God
in the mid-day sun.
I imagined I was glorious, magnificent,
omnipotent –
worthy even of my own worship.

But this far from safe passage,
my ship thrown upon the waves,
I am humbled:
humiliated by frail mortality.

Here, this failing body is mine.
This tensed hand,
with its red-mottled weathered skin,
is all I am.
This rope which tears my flesh,
is my god. Without it,
I am clawing empty air, praying
that these grey mountains of stormy water
will wash away the last remnants of the day.

2.

The angels hear nothing.
Underneath copper cascades of Botticelli hair,
their dainty ears are plugged with sealing wax.

My penitence therefore is not worth a damn.

Angels, hear me!

My words are fools that tread through muddy fields
where you will not go. *Hear me!*
My boat is water-logged, sodden, about to go down.
Let your golden coins, like your golden tears,
fall down from heaven.
Let them descend with me, to the lightless depths
where I shall forever lie, crucified upon the ocean floor.

Angels, hear me!

Take off your flowing gowns and rub my face
in the soft folds of your mothering pudenda.
Let the lord of delight pull back the curtains of his disgust,
for I cannot remain hidden or chewed up by lust.
Give me the cup of your labial lips that I may drink,
for I am wretched with my thirst.

Angels, hear me!

Bring your shining nails: pierce me with your purity;
castigate & revile me, for I am nothing, but a driftwood whore
floating on a sea of decay.

Angels, hear me!

I cry out, but the angels cannot hear me:
my prayers fall, answerless, into the echoing void.

3.

There are angels in this dead head:
virgin warriors dancing through
dreams of sleep;
through bellied clouds,
the texture of moon-blood.
They are skin, flesh, bone,
atomic structure: cold as forged metal,
brutally perfect.
I envy the sunlight that plays
upon their hair,
adore their untouchable presence...
       but want to touch them all the same.

Imagine then, a post-coital haze,
wrapped in the tender arms of an angel:
her breasts, milk-soft
against the hard edges of my back;
the feather down of her hair
coiled in my lazy fingers;
her kisses, shaky and bursting
on the back of my neck.

4.

In the belly of this wrecked ship I wait for salvation.
Saint Paul lays trembling, thou-shalt-not hands upon me.
He would heal my soul with meat-hooks
and tender instruments of torture;
and carve the scriptures into my skin.
He only knows the benediction of fire.
As without, so within.

Lay your brands upon me father,
for I have laughed with too many Liliths;
and now I dream only of angel quim.

Lay your hands upon me
and take me down into the deep,
that I may succumb to eternal sleep.
Take me down, gentle Jesus,
as a lamb to your shambles yard.
Brace my head in a cobbled lock;
and take your steely blade,
swift and sweet,
to this petitioning flesh.

Down, down, down,
I descend into the netherworld:
beyond the cloying reach of clinical hands.
I will not be saved by anything less than pain.
Innanna, these diamonds are dust:
let me sing for you again.

Vision Of The Drowning Man

1. Asylum

Into the dark cloud,
into this sodden shroud
of bruised pearl drops,
spinning,
a vortex of woven rain,
petrol spectres,
oil soaked rainbows.

His ship is wrecked,
wretched
and storm tossed.
The bilges are clogged,
the sails soiled,
the ropes strained
to snapping point.

Lashed by acid spindrift,
he clutches bilious hands
and prays
for safe passage.

*Oh mother, oh angels,
hear me!* he cries,
but they hear him not.

The waves
pregnant with the mystery
of dead babies,
his face pressed
into a mesh
of cabled steel,
salt rotted grooves
in ancient flesh —
an albatross
dangling from his neck.

He crouches on the deck,
spirals in starboard arcs
of penitence.

Help me, he cries,
the dark mother goddess
has pissed on my bonfire
and all the stars have conspired
to cast me down
into the lowest reaches
of hell.

*   *   *

Down down
into the soulless abyss,
into the lightless void
where there is wailing
and gnashing of teeth,
where the witch's blade
cuts nothing from nothing,
and out of nothing
nothing is re-made.

His dreams are of
atoms disintegrating,
the subtle shifts
of entropy,
the emptiness
in the eyes
of everyone else,
the hell
of other people,
particles –
diamonds reduced to carbon,
worlds swallowed by Abaddon.

Ariadne doesn't dare enter
the dark chambers
of his nightmares.
There is no Innanna
willing to suffer
the conspiracy of love.

He is doomed
to shipwrecked solitude,
dashing his fists
against padded walls
till the fire is burned out
and the darkness

has reduced him
to meek compliance.

       *   *   *

There are angels
in the dead-end corridors
of his deadened brain,
they dance in dreams of sleep
through sticky, viscous cloud,
the texture of moon-blood,
the taste of salt and rust
burnt deep into
the fibres of his tongue.

The angels in his dead head
dance on tightropes of razorwire –
their perfect flesh, blue as ether,
cold as the rainbow's edge.

They mean no harm,
in their laughing innocence.

Down he goes,
down on them,
each and every one,
lapping up
the quintessence of quim,
an impudent tongue
cleaving velvet pudenda.

Down he goes,
down into saturated clouds,
a shroud of silk
smothering the ravaged lines
of his slowly exploding face.

Down he goes,
down into netherworld,
riding the dying swan –
falling beyond
the cloying grasp
of clinical hands,
through strands of madness
the barbiturates cannot touch.

This is too much, he raves, *too much,*
in this too white, white silence,
his catatonic flesh resisting
in spasms of ultraviolence.

He is drowning
in narcotic milk,
going down,
down,
        down

an obscene litany
rattling round
his head —

I go down on you, Kali Ma,
dark goddess,
I drink deep
of your holy depths,
succumb
to the undying ecstasy
of your perfect despair.

Whip me!
Pierce me!
For I am rotten fruit —
chaffed, not sweet,
goat, not sheep —
a blasphemous offering
on your blood stained altar,
an abomination,
an abortion.

Discard me!
Cast me into your burning pit,
torch my ship,
undo me.

Let me dream along
of being born
again.

      *   *   *

Down down down,
this steering wheel spins round,
a spinning wheel
knitting nothing
from nothing –
he knows
what goes up comes down
and what comes around
goes around.

He has cast the twenty-two cards
too many times
to be blinded
by impermanence.

Yet there's an acid fleck
in his conviction,
a corrosive presence
in his house –
a ghost who laughs
with mocking, rotten teeth,
a mineshaft beneath the street,
the pavement cracking
and a yawning chasm
yawning underneath.

    *   *   *

Over in the locked wards
birds fly round vacated heads,
a dry mouth chants
the names of ex-lovers,
*Sylvia, Maria, Celestine,
Anna, Martha, Christine...*

Dear sweet Christ,
What the fuck is happening?

z. Beyond The Asylum

Down The Meadows,
the wind rips
pink and cream blossom
from tentative trees,
cuts jagged knives
through naked ribs,
vicious as Hibs casuals
on a psychopathic Saturday night.

Plugged into this machine,
I'm safe: a radio ghost, a spectre
of industrial dance,
a hundred and twenty beats
to each disappearing minute,
my feet moving,
each after the other,
automatic
over the tarmac,
weaving through a blur
of pedestrian insanity –
       I can't bear to look,
to see, to feel, to hear
the sad, fucked up stories,
the Breugal expanses
painted on pained,
grey-ingrained faces.
       This cat walks alone,
eyes screwed to skewed slits –
the wind tries to speak,
tries to breach
the walls
of my resistance.

Hunched up on a bread crate,
huddled in scabby blankets,
a young bedraggled couple,
rainwet and shivering,
beg for sustenance
from passers-by:
Help the homeless, the girl says,
an impersonal plea
with an impersonal voice,
like her need was an abstraction.

This cat walks alone,
this cat strides by, not looking,
not listening:
this cat, bop-walking
to techno trance,
a million DJ gods
in the aural caves
that twist and spiral
into the core of his brain,
throbbing and thumping,
pumping adrenal virtual sex
through fibrous veins
of virtual unreality;
this cat untouched,
unmoved
by homeless children,
he strides up
the Middle Meadow Walk,
through green pastures,
into the anonymous chaos
of labyrinthine city streets.

* * *

Along the Forest Road
I weave a tangled, jerky web
through a minefield
of overgrown, too well-fed,
private-school children,
blue-blazered, loud-mouthed
and well spoken,
past blazing shops
and shadowy doorways,
through the affluence
and the effluent
of this city's
dull dreaming.

* * *

Jesus Christ! Fuck!
Look at this, I mean to say,
what the fuck?
What the fuck
is it all about?
Fucking bastard!
Fucking cunt!

City dreams and dust.
The thunderbirds are gone:
they've laid waste
to the dreaming spires
of Eldorado,
slain the monks
of Buckfast Abbey
and washed their bones
in purple methanol.

An old wino, collapsed
in grey-stained paralysis,
her ripped frock
draining a yellow stream
of steaming urine,
blurring
on the rainwet pavement,
an unspoken panic
in the lines of her face:
she who lay down
like a little lamb
for a can of Carlie.

* * *

This cat can find no shadows to skulk in,
no respite from the glare of the moon,
no place to hide from her brilliance,
her vehemence.

See! she screams,
hurling thunderbolts
through the silence
of white noise,
cutting lines from the pulse
of pumped up volume,
of kicked out jams,
of technological trance –
left of the leftfield,
underneath the underworld,
she defines an orbit
of the orbital: this orb,
this holy, white globe.
She is ubiquitous,
iniquitous,
cannot be shunned,
for even a stopped clock
tells the right time
twice a day.

3. Greyfriars Cemetery

The dead emanate a stony tranquillity,
muffling the roar of the city –
their stories quietly erased,
faded out
like forgotten inscriptions,
and even the wee scabby dog
rests in peace,
now that the tourists
are departed.

The oak is naked,
raw and black
it reaches up to a fruitless sky.

I remember
when we were young enough
to chase falling leaves,
believing in their power
to bestow upon us
the granting of our wishes;

and I wonder now
did your wishes
come true?

Did you not once say
you wanted to get to a place
that was beyond caring,
beyond the here and now?

Oh, how the universe
has mocked you!

Even amongst the dead
I cannot find the peace I seek –
your emptied out eyes
stare at me from the clouds,
accusing me of cowardice.

It's true,
I didn't follow you,
my mad saviour.

I never got to dance in heaven.
I bailed out
when your ship went sailing
into the wild ocean –
I clung to the soil
and you waved goodbye,
left me harbour bound,
helplessly watching
the wanton wind
ripping the sails
and the rigging
from your craft.

Here, amongst the dead,
here, on dry land,
I feel the magma boiling up
under the thin crust
of this dry earth
and I thirst
for the cataclysm
that will wipe us all out.

I am sick of caring –
I yearn to be wrenched out
of this anxious existence,
to melt into the cosmos
and scatter my atoms
like radioactive dust.

I'm listening out
for the trumpets
and the timpani,
for the seven angels
of the apocalypse –
I'm waiting
for the end
of all this wanting,
all this needing.

Here, amongst the dead,
lying in the lank grass,
watching your blank eyes
in the blank clouds
I'm praying for peace –
an end to all this suffering,
an end to all this

me me me,
an end
to the quiet insanity
of being.

Here, amongst the stones,
amongst the bones of the dead
I've come to understand
the wisdom of the Buddha,
but I cannot find that peace
which surpasses mere understanding.

4. Leith Walk

The moon is lost behind a gridlock of clouds —
I feel her stirring my psyche
with her pale, probing fingers,
pulling back my eyelids
so that I must *see*.

She comes to me in whispers,
in tarot spreads,
in dreams of love
that wake me sweating
from her tender and cruel touch —
she is too much.

She has saturated the blood
of lovers and family,
shifted the furniture
that lies behind their eyes.

Everywhere the moon follows me,
even into the bright skies
of mid-day:
she is with me
every step of the way.

5. Bonnington

The spey wife, in her Bonnington sanctuary,
with her crystals, incense, Afghan rugs,
portrait of the Queen above the mantelpiece,
nick-nacks and tat from Scarborough, Brighton
and Brightlingsea –
she stared deep into the heart of me,
unnerved me.

The moon has got into your soul son,
she's sharpened up her knife
and is readying
to pare you to the bone –
do not resist!
She'll open you up,
wide as the mother mouth
of Sheila Na Gig.
She'll play with you,
tease you, taunt you
and love you too,
visiting upon you
the blessing
and the curse
of her vision.

The spey wife, in the safety
of her Bonnington sitting room,
with her crystals, incense, psychic eyes,
photo of Sai Baba on the wall,
nick-nacks and tat from Rishikesh,
Haridwar and Dharamsala –
she laid her hot hands on my cold stomach,
unnerved me.

See, my wee laddie,
your chakras are spinning
like Morningside dafties
running round the town.
We need to close them down,
rein in these wild flowers
before they turn to seed –
you need
to soak your feet
in the salt earth.

The spey wife, floating
above the spiky chimneys
of Edinburgh's skyline: a tear
for every unimagined story,
a shredded crystal embedded
in the black temple
of her all-seeing eyes.
The spey wife, the woman who knows,
seeing deep into my soul,
unnerving me, rearranging me,
filling my hollow belly
with the moon's warm glow.

6. North Berwick

Witches were drowned here,
riding the rip-tide
in cinnamon boats
with blood-red sails.

I think of you,
magus of the underworld,
drowning
in hospital linen,
white
as a swan's feather.

Like you, I am adrift,
out on the margins
with my crystals,
my tarot pack
and my shiny, spinning,
too open chakras.

I am rudderless —
must navigate
both storm and calm
without a map —
only the fickle moon
to guide me.

I came out here
to soak myself
in winter rain
and spindrift,
to shake the city grime
from my hair,
but still
I see your blank eyes
staring down at me
from the blank clouds.

    *   *   *

Breathing in the salt earth,
I feel almost atoned –
stoned by the silence
of the waves
washing over my feet,
cold fish
weaving webs
around my toes,
anchoring me
to the dark currents
of inevitability.

I am there in your hospital room
and I am here in the sea,
wishing I was a fisher of men –
a gentle Jesus,
able to cast out my net
and haul you back in.

Afterword

One of the things that most leftfield/experimental poets have to put up with is the constant questioning about the "meaning" of their poetry. The questioners, in my experience, seem to feel that the poet has been wilfully obscure, or even elitist, that they are doing the cerebral equivalent of showing off in the playground, a sort of literary breakdancing.

I can't speak for other poets, except to say that I believe that most poets are singularly and sincerely dedicated to their craft, and that if they wanted to indulge in intellectual masturbation, they would chose another, more popular medium. Poetry is, after all, the sick man of the arts, and few poets can command the sort of audiences that would make such showing off worthwhile.

I am aware that the poetry in this particular collection is probably my least accessible to date. I have not made it intentionally so. Writing for me is a method of exploring; and with these poems I went off exploring, without a map. It was an adventure, exploring the outer fringes of uncharted territory; and I delighted in it. It doesn't matter what these poems mean. Let them mean whatever they mean to you; disengage the part of your brain that was erroneously, but not irreversibly, hardwired during dull years of English literature studies at school or – if you were unlucky enough – at university.

To me – the writer – these poems are both complex and simple, like an acid trip. They are also completely lucid. But then again, I am in a very privileged position. I have all the passwords to the locked compartments in my head. You, as a reader, only have a map covered with hieroglyphs. Maybe some of these symbols will resonate for you, maybe not. It very much depends where you are coming from and where you have been. If you have trodden some of the roads I've walked, my poetry won't be so obscure to you. If you've taken hallucinogenic drugs; if you've travelled in Asia; if you dig underground music; if you have read way out literature; if you've been unemployed or homeless; if you've ever slumped in despair; if you've ever danced all night right through to sunrise; if you've made it into your forties and are still dreaming; if you've ever wished you could wave a magic wand and make the world a better place; if you've ever laughed at a tragedy or cried at a joke; and if after all that you still don't know what you want to be, then the chances are you'll have some idea of where I'm coming from.

Dee Sunshine

Acknowledgements

Autumn In Florence was published in *Liminal Pleasures* #1 (Italy, 2006).

The Swimmer And She Who Knows was published in *Terrible Work* #9 (England, 1999).

An early draft of **Black Night/ Pink Gin** was published in *Dada Dance* #2 (Scotland, 1986)

Bitten Back Words was published in *Fire And Reason*, Vol 2 #1, (Canada, 2000)

A Rain Of Roses was published in *Liminal Pleasures* #1, (Italy, 2006) and *Vallum* Vol 4 #1, (Canada, 2006)

Holes was published in *Riot Angel* #1 (England, 2004).

An early draft of **In Thrall To Lilith** was published in *Vigil* #16 (England, 2000) and *Acid Angel* #3 (Scotland, 2000) and a later draft was published in *Riot Angel* #1 (England, 2004).

The Blood Of Christ was published in *Acid Angel* #3 (Scotland, 2000) and in *Spume* #1 (Scotland, 2002) and it has appeared in two anthologies: *In Our Own Words* Volume 4 (MWE publications, USA, 2002); and *Mind Mutations* (Sun Rising Poetry Press, USA, 2005).

An early draft of **Days Gone By** was published in *Spume* #1 (Scotland, 2002) and a later draft was published in *Erbacce* #1 (England, 2004).

Slugging For Sweet Jesus was published in *Acid Angel* #3 (Scotland, 2000) and in *Neon Highway* #6 (England, 2003).

Narcissus was published in *Erbacce* #2 (England, 2005).

Heavy Weather was published in the anthology *Letting Go Of The Earth* (Be Strong Press, Wales, 1999).

NB: Most of these publications were credited under my previous name, Dee Rimbaud, and some were published under the pseudonym Yoshi Ooshi.

About The Author

Dee Sunshine is an artist, writer, musician and new age gypsy. He has been on the road, travelling in Europe and Asia since 2006. He is the author of two poetry collections, *The Bad Seed* (Stride, 1998) and *Dropping Ecstasy With The Angels* (Bluechrome, 2004); and one novel, *Stealing Heaven From The Lips Of God* (Bluechrome, 2004). He edited the charity poetry anthology, *The Book Of Hopes And Dreams* (Bluechrome, 2006) and edited the AA Independent Press Guide from 1998-2011. His art has appeared in hundreds of literary magazines and on the book covers of poetry collections by Janet Buck, Clarinda Harriss, Rupert Loydell, Norman Jope among others. Reproductions of his art are now available from Red Bubble at http://www.redbubble.com/people/deesunshine. You can read more of Dee's poetry and see more of his art on his website at www.thunderburst.co.uk

If you want to get in touch with Dee he welcomes email enquiries: shooglemail@googlemail.com

www.ingramcontent.com/pod-product-compliance
Lightning Source LLC
Chambersburg PA
CBHW022136080426
42734CB00006B/392